C0-BFU-351

WITHDRAWN

DAVIS WASHINGTON MITCHELL LECTURES
TULANE UNIVERSITY

The American University in the Twentieth Century

By William Clyde DeVane

CHRISTIAN COLLEGE LIBRARY
COLUMBIA, MISSOURI

LOUISIANA STATE UNIVERSITY PRESS
BATON ROUGE

V

Copyright 1957
BY THE LOUISIANA STATE UNIVERSITY PRESS

Library of Congress Card Catalog Number: 57-7496

Manufactured in the United States of America
BY THE WILLIAM BYRD PRESS, INC.
RICHMOND, VIRGINIA

18317 83

Foreword

❖

IN 1954 Mrs. Ida Mitchell Looney a native of New Orleans, and a resident of Dallas, established in Tulane University the Davis Washington Mitchell Fund in memory of her grandfather. This Fund is to provide annually, or as near annually as feasible, a series of lectures to be known as the Davis Washington Mitchell Lectures, dealing with subjects "Stimulative of independent thought and gracious living, and which may increase devotion to the public good," which qualities characterized the life and career of Davis Washington Mitchell, a Louisiana planter.

The first series of lectures was presented by William Clyde DeVane, Sanford Professor of English and Dean of Yale College on March 22, 23, 26 and 27, 1956. Tulane University was pleased to have present at the lectures the donor of the Davis Washington Mitchell Fund. In establishing this series, Mrs. Looney wisely placed little restriction on their topics. They are a tribute to the memory of a sensitive, cultured man and the quest for a way of life that is good. It is the same way of life the intelligent man of Western civilization has sought since the advent of classical civilization. The lectures are a tribute to a man who treasured that older day of richer, quieter and more contemplative living. The qualities of the good life which came from that day may contribute more than appears on the surface to the handling of the problems of our time.

❖

Preface

❖

IN MARCH 1956 I had the honor of inaugurat-
ing the newly-endowed Davis Washington
Mitchell Lectures at Tulane University. To Tulane,
and to the donor of the lectureship, I am profoundly
grateful for the honor, and for the opportunity it
gave me to examine with a Southern audience the
subject of American higher education in the twentieth century. As a member of the Board of Trustees
of the General Education Board and as a Southerner
by birth I have been especially interested in the rise
to national stature of the universities of the South
in recent years, especially the independent universities of the Southeast and central South. In these
institutions, and in a few excellent colleges and an
increasingly strong system of state universities, we
have good auguries for the future of education in
the South, as the whole region rouses itself from its

dreams of the past and faces a hopeful future. In the new era of prosperity in the South, in the demands of its increasingly complex industrial society for thoughtful, trained men and women, and perhaps above all in the democratic principle of fuller educational opportunity for all, it is clear that the public universities are going to be flooded and perhaps overwhelmed by numbers of students. It will be the challenging opportunity of the privately endowed institutions to set standards and maintain quality. Such institutions as Tulane, I believe, are on the brink of their most prosperous and useful era. My comments are therefore directed toward such independent and privately endowed universities, and only glance in passing at the major portion of the two thousand educational institutes, colleges, and special schools beyond high school that make up our huge and complex educational system.

These four lectures—which I have made no attempt to recast into essays—look much to the past, for I believe that each educational institution worthy of the name has its own genius, a special quality of place and time that it must foster, which grew in the first instance out of the aspirations of the community that produced it, and like a tree with deep roots, its growth and shape must be largely controlled by the temper and quality, the climate of opinion, of the community and, beyond it, the nation from which it gets its life and strength. The past of these many great universities has a natural diversity, but also much that is common. In the course of these lectures I make some strong, but I think justified, claims for the importance of such universities to our national health. From them have come, and will come in increasing numbers, the leaders in our industrial, political, economic, scientific, cultural, and spiritual life.

William C. DeVane

Table of Contents

• • xi • •

THE AMERICAN UNIVERSITY
IN THE TWENTIETH CENTURY

The University—Its Scope
and Function

IT WAS just 104 years ago that Cardinal Newman formulated for Irish and Catholic young
men his *Idea of a University*. Among his large conceptions and noble utterances there is one that un-
dertakes to describe the function and purpose of a
university education: "A University training is the
great ordinary means to a great but ordinary end:
it aims at raising the intellectual tone of society, at
cultivating the public mind, at purifying the national taste, at supplying true principles to popular
enthusiasm and fixed aims to popular aspiration, at
giving enlargement and sobriety to the ideas of the
age, at facilitating the exercise of political powers,
and refining the intercourse of private life." It is
true here that Newman narrows his comment to
"University training," but it is clear from the context, I think, that he recognizes only the teaching

function of the university which is indeed central, but as we shall see is by no means the whole task which the modern university sets for itself.

There are many other remarks to be made about Newman's passage. Perhaps we notice first the emphasis which Newman puts upon the word *ordinary*—by which I infer that he means that such an education is worldly, for the purposes of the secular world, and that he has in mind higher studies, such as theology, for higher purposes. But even at the secular and worldly level he is setting up ideals for such an education as we have not been able to accomplish—they are large and generous conceptions, and goals that no college or university within my knowledge has been fully able to achieve in our time, especially in its immediate effect upon its community or society. It is fairly evident that Newman is thinking of an idealized and purified Oxford, an Oxford not of his own youth but rather of his dreams, and also of an Oxford in its collegiate aspects rather than the University—an Oxford that had its chief social effects through the training of the individual in close and intimate instruction. His idea embodies the finer genius and the remembered essence of Oxford.

There is one surprising difference that you may have noticed between Newman's *Idea* and the modern American university. It is all the difference between a college and a university. The primary aim of Newman's university is to teach the "diffusion and extension of knowledge rather than the advancement. If its object were scientific and philosophical discovery, I do not see why a University should have students." Newman seems to have no notion that a university can train an investigator, and he naïvely relegates the task of increasing learning to institutions and academies. His aim is to fit the student, in point of information, intelligence, and manners, for the world, not for the laboratory and the library. There is no real appreciation of the scientific method and temper which have informed our modern universities, nor is there any provision for revealing "the grand development of human reason, from Aristotle down to Hegel." In short, Newman's ideals were the collegiate and rather static ideals of the great English and American institutions of a century ago, however dim their lights and unimpressive their achievements, and they had not yet envisaged the university idea that was even in Newman's time being born in Germany.

I need not dwell at this point at any length upon the amazing development of the American university in the last half of the nineteenth century. It is a well-known story. But a few observations may be of interest. In great numbers, our scholars in all fields went to Germany for their training and brought back home many Germanic or Continental ideas of a university which in many respects ran

· · 5 · ·

somewhat counter to our traditional English and American ideas. Not only was German education more thorough, especially at the higher levels, but its scope was immensely vaster. Its ideal was not the English and American ideal—to produce a gentleman capable of taking his place in Church and Civil State. Its aim was altogether more practical, more bourgeois, more professional. It featured the great professor giving great lectures and having little else to do with the students beyond examining them to test their professional competence. It featured the library, the laboratory, and research. It insisted upon the advancement of knowledge and the publication of dissertations, abstracts, monographs, and papers. It exalted the monolithic professor to a pitch which our present egalitarian civilization would not tolerate. We remember the Herr Geheimrat Professor who thought so well of himself that every time he mentioned himself he raised his hat. With some ridiculous features, and some that have become abhorrent to us, we must admit that the German accomplishment in the nineteenth century was epoch making, and revolutionized the process and the conception of learning and culture in the Western world. To a degree hitherto unfamiliar the Germans professionalized learning. Though in its early rise in the nineteenth century the German university devoted its primary attention to those studies which we usually designate as the Humanities—literature, philosophy, history, and religion—perhaps its greatest accomplishment was to establish on impregnable bases the new sciences—chemistry, biology, medicine—but they did not neglect the older interests of learning, such as the higher criticism of the Scriptures, the classics, and archaeology. Their effect was happier in the sciences, perhaps, where they had a new and clear field. Their methods in the older fields, while fruitful of good intellectual results, sometimes forgot their humane nature and the true nature of their value to society.

At any rate, the effect of German learning and culture upon America was profound. Mainly in this tradition a whole host of new universities was born in this country. Not only such magnificent new institutions as The Johns Hopkins University, Cornell University (where it was the ideal of the founder that any student might study any subject), the University of Chicago, and California and Stanford on the West Coast, but a handsome array of state universities rose to take their places in the great new system. Significantly, too, the older institutions of the East Coast began the slow, hard process of transforming themselves from colleges into universities, absorbing into the new conception of their function their famous colleges. Since they were not new foundations and had much that they valued, their tasks were often harder. But we see the growing pains of Harvard in Eliot's regime—his adoption of the elective system is one of them—and of Yale in the establishment of the Sheffield Scientific School as a separate entity. These two institutions, and along with them Columbia, as the century wore on, gradually added or refurbished their advanced schools of law, medicine, divinity, and their graduate schools. In 1861 Yale awarded the first Doctor of Philosophy degree in America, and the modern age was in sight. Though still living in the shadow of Europe, the American universities were coming of age, and at the end of the century so competent and acute an observer as Lord Bryce could say: ". . . I will say that while of all the institutions of the country [the universities] are those of which Americans speak most modestly, and indeed deprecatingly, they are those which seem to be at this moment making the swiftest progress, and have the brightest promise for the future. They are supplying exactly those things which European critics have hitherto found lacking to America; and they are contributing to her political as well as to her contemplative life elements of inestimable worth."

These are kind and flattering words, but candor compels us to say that the universities of America of 1900 were not adequate to the society of that time. It is true that the major lines had been laid down. At the base was the college, and beyond were the major schools of law, medicine, letters and science, and sometimes divinity. But of what relatively poor quality, and of what distorted shapes and proportions these schools were, we can see with the advantage of hindsight. As an example of the quality, or lack of it, I need only point out Flexner's great reform of the schools of medicine later in our century. As an example of the distortion in conception I need only cite the lack of a base at Johns Hopkins and the lack of an adequate one for a time at Chicago. Moreover, our higher schools were immature and derivative, and were following models which were made in Europe and drawing their most distinguished professors from abroad. In 1900 we were only beginning to totter on our own feet. Some parts of our country were even less well provided with adequate institutions of higher learning. The South, slowly recovering from the War between the States, could not afford the great and complete universities which it badly needed. But decade by decade in the twentieth century our great institutions have become more mature and native, and the end is not yet. On our reluctant assumption of world leadership after the Second World War our institutions of higher education in America have had forced upon them the responsibility for guarding the quality and nature of learning of our Western culture. We are no longer the colonials, but the mother country, and this emphasis will increase. Will we be equal to the challenge?

The demands upon our institutions of higher learning in America are only equalled by the touching faith of the country in education, a faith which has not yet materialized in sufficient money to sustain our vast, indeed perhaps our impossible, ambitions. Our universities are put in the position of being the brains, the heart, and the conscience of our society. Our scientists and engineers are called upon to ensure the security of the nation; they are expected to provide the ideas which keep industry alive and moving; our social scientists are largely responsible for the economic welfare of the country, the effectiveness of our political and social organization, the ideas informing our relations with other nations; our great medical centers are entrusted not only with the health of the country but are expected to provide more adequately for the future by their discoveries to the end that pain and disease may be eliminated or reduced; our humanists are responsible before the world for our moral and spiritual health, the quality of our ethical, critical, and creative thought in history, letters, philosophy, and religion. The demands upon us are far ahead of our social development, both in quantity and quality. Our country wants and needs liberal education for our young people as a base upon which they may specialize, but seldom understands why the base is necessary, and is inclined to think it merely a matter of prestige. Still, something is happening. Not many years ago the degrees of bachelor of arts and science were thought of as terminal degrees. Nowadays about sixty per cent of the graduates of many of our Eastern colleges go on to advanced degrees in the higher schools of the universities. But the hunger of society for trained men and women is not appeased.

Now in spite of the immense value which society is slowly coming to place upon the university as one of its major secular institutions, it is not possible to be complacent about the situation. We live in a society that is pragmatic, opportunistic, materialistic, and fundamentally anti-intellectual. The professor is the butt of innumerable jokes, none of them flattering to him. When he endeavors to participate in public life he often becomes in the public mind a national menace. Ten years after our students graduate from our colleges they come back to reunions (having been immersed in American life), poorer intellectually, emotionally, and spiritually than when they left us a decade earlier. And there are dangers which even now imperil such efficiency as we have. To begin with a relatively small point, the government and industry are in danger of using up our "seed-corn"—that is, of drawing off from the universities by their immense material rewards the great teachers and men of ideas. By these developments not only will the flow of well-trained men coming out of the universities diminish, but the seminal home of pure, disinterested research is in danger of being impoverished. But that is a danger that can be met. More importantly, the demands of the society upon the universities are often injudicious and ill-considered and, in my opinion, should not be met. We ought to draw a firm, clear line. We ought to do those things which we are well qualified to do, and have resources to do well. We ought to confine ourselves and our activities to the conduct of schools and departments where the training of the intellect is the most important aspect. Already our universities have become warped out of shape by the demands of society for physical education, schools of hotel management, advertising and commercial schools, schools of nursing and journalism, and many much worse marginal affairs. Those activities, worthy enough in themselves perhaps, where techniques overwhelm history and theory, ought to be left to special separate institutions, and are not of immediate concern to the university. This, I am aware, is to draw an arbitrary and fine line. Where should our service to the nation cease? Rather, phrase the question differently, and ask what the universities can do that no other institutions can do, things that will not be done unless the universities do them. These are the matters of the intellect—the true higher learning. We ought to limit our ambitions for service to the society and raise our quality of performance in those things we undertake. We ought to aim to be admired rather than to be popular. There is room enough for us if we aim to preserve, perpetuate, and advance learning, and prepare men and women for the great professions. No doubt, special schools will rise to take care of the secondary needs of our society, but they would generally be better left out of the university structure.

For the university has a larger and more important task than merely being the *immediate* servant of society. It needs to stand somewhat apart, though deeply concerned; to be the severe but friendly critic of the society; to raise the intellectual tone of the society; to be the arbiter of public taste; to call its attention to reason and principle; to keep the culture of the nation in balance; to remind the people of their history, their ancient ideals of freedom and justice; to guard their spiritual state. To do these things well will not only take all the material resources at our disposal; it will take character and courage and a strong reliance upon principle to meet the incessant demands that beat upon our gates. For institutions have certain human qualities. They are ambitious, greedy, and lustful of power. They are vain and compliant, and wish too eagerly to please. But then, too, we must not forget that universities, in their best feature, are companies of scholars, and are the finest representatives of American culture in all its most reasonable and altruistic aspects.

The universities also have social characters and personalities, as one can sense who travels from, let us say, Harvard to Columbia, from Yale to Michigan, to say nothing of moving from Tulane to California. And this brings me to what I regard as a very important matter. To be genuinely effective, a university must be a community and have a corporate spirit. Several considerations come in at this point. Possibly sheer size does not *prohibit* such a community, but it obviously makes cohesion and co-operation difficult. Location is another consideration. The university in a gigantic city finds it very difficult to draw its faculty together into a community of scholars, and suffers also from the danger that its students may be overwhelmingly local. Columbia struggles against both of these disadvantages, and Harvard has constantly to be on guard against Boston. On the other hand, the university in the woods is constantly threatened by intellectual anemia unless it has very considerable resources to bring the world of ideas to its doors; and if the community is too tight and close in a small town there is the danger of complacency and excessive conformity.

In America we are infatuated by bigness, and the tendency of our society is towards larger and larger units. No doubt, that makes for efficiency and a kind of mass standard which in most everyday matters is fairly good. Standardization and conformity are the price we pay for our material benefits. But education is not a commodity of this material kind; it is rather the awakening of the mind and spirit of the individual—of give and take, of person to person, of scholar to student, of scholar to scholar, and of the lonely original scholar in the library or the laboratory. For these reasons, I think there is an optimum size to a university, and there are optimum conditions—say, a university of seven to eight thousand in all, established on the edge of a middle-sized city which is not too far removed from the main currents of contemporary thought and culture.

Now in the great rush of students which is almost at our doors the great state universities will be almost helpless to protect themselves, and many of them which have won distinction as communities of scholars and students—communities, each with a personality and a character of its own—will be in grave danger of being distorted and battered out of shape, of being overrun and harried until they lose all sense of direction and quality. It will be squarely up to the independently endowed and privately supported institutions, such as Tulane, Duke, Emory, and Vanderbilt in the South, and the older institutions in the East, to continue to do their national duty, as I see it, to protect the standards and strive for the ideal community of scholars and students. I need not remind you that the task will be a very difficult one indeed.

To hark back now to Newman's conception of a hundred years ago is to see its many limitations. He was in truth speaking of a college, of a teaching and training institution, and a small one at that, modeled somewhat on what he had experienced at Oxford. What he saw as the sole function of such an institution is still an important one—the training of an important group of students in the moral and intellectual virtues—perhaps the most important one for America in our time. But since Newman's day a very great deal has happened. We have had, it is not too much to say, a series of revolutions. The Industrial Revolution has developed apace. The Scientific Revolution has had, and is still having, an immense effect upon our modes of thinking and the everyday details of our life. The democratic processes in society, which were in their infancy a hundred years ago, have made the present age one of the common man. Accompanying these new forces, there has risen a sharper sense of nationalism which has profoundly affected the scope and direction of learning itself—to the extent of curbing its freedom and its universal nature. The world has changed, and the demands of society upon the university have been enormously enlarged. The university now must not only be the repository of learning and the perpetuator of learning through its teaching function; it has also the immense responsibility of creating new knowledge, both for the preservation of the nation which now has the most independent of universities, and for the health and sanity of our national culture.

The functions of our educational institutions have expanded with the growth and complexity of our nation. The primary function of our early colonial colleges, to train men for the Church and Civil State, is still central in a modified form. To that conception we have added the notion that the university is the repository of our heritage, as may be seen in our vast libraries and museums. Further, we have assumed the tremendous task of advancing knowledge of all kinds. The process of specialization has entered into the structure of modern society, and in the division of labor the university has become the brains of the community and the nation. Beyond that, the university has to a considerable degree become the custodian of the society's health and spirit—its sanity and balance. Though we remain critics of the society which supports us, our fate is inextricably bound up with that society. We are in the market place with mankind to a degree rarely seen before in the history of the world. The ivory tower is a term of the past.

The College

For all their variety and number—now more than twelve hundred—the four-year American college leading to the bachelor's degree is a native adaptation of the English idea of higher education. Taking their origins from the collegiate schools of seventeenth-century New England and Virginia, they have spread like a prairie fire across the land. It is a strange fact that our collegiate system in America was established before there was an adequate secondary school system to sustain it—for all the world like a real estate development far out on the edges of a hopeful town, with streets and sidewalks, but without as yet very many inhabitants or houses. It is a poor state that does not now have a dozen collegiate institutions within its borders. They have varied so in size, purpose, curriculum, and quality that one may think they have little in common in our day.

But certain qualities and habits persist in our young people and are common to all. During his tenure as president of Yale College the Reverend Ezra Stiles sounded a note which may still be heard in the land. He said ". . . a hundred and fifty or a hundred and eighty Young Gentlemen students is a bundle of Wildfire not easily controlled and governed—and at best the Diadem of a president is a Crown of Thorns." The presidents have succeeded in shifting the Crown of Thorns to the deans in the course of time, but the thorns are perennial. I would remind you of the other side. It was this same president Stiles, perhaps with a touch of unexpected and wry humor, who taught his senior students Hebrew because he was reluctant to have his boys go to Heaven and not know the language of the place. The care for what happens to the students goes on, too.

To speak of American colleges in all their variety is too huge a task for discussion here, and I have set a limit upon myself by directing my remarks to only a portion of them—that is, to the colleges embedded in the modern American universities. That is a wide enough field, to be sure, but this group does have features and problems in common, certain advantages and certain restrictions upon its operation which are not usually to be found in the colleges independent of universities. The most salient difference, perhaps, is that the colleges embedded in universities have had to adapt themselves to a Continental or German conception of higher education which has prevailed in most universities. For all that, our colleges, both within universities and separate, are possibly the most native of our institutions. On one side, they are not the Lycées of France or the Hochschulen of Germany, or the English public schools, such as Eton and Harrow. Nor, on the other side, are they the vocationally and professionally oriented universities of the Continent. They come nearest to Oxford and Cambridge in their great goal of providing a *Studium Generale*—in providing an advanced stage of general studies as a broad, humane, and integrated preparation for life, the object being to make the student transform *himself* into a more real, more substantial, more three-dimensional person. But they rarely carry the student as far as Oxford and Cambridge, and increasingly the modern undergraduate feels it necessary to supplement his bachelor's degree with further work in a professional or graduate school.

In point of time, our colleges were established first for the most part, and only gradually grew up into universities. In contrast to this general rule, Cornell, as we shall see, sprang fully armed from the head of Andrew D. White, and Johns Hopkins began as a graduate school. In 1900 the populations of our largest colleges were small, and only in recent years have the great offices in government, industry, and civic life been held by college-bred men. The first great wave of students came to the colleges in the Twenties—after the First World War —and except briefly in the Second World War the wave has never receded, even during the Depression. The prospect now is that by 1965 our present college population will be doubled—and that is a staggering thought—for more and more the complexity of our civilization demands the bachelor's degree at the minimum, and the socially inclined as well as those eager for success use the college degree as a ladder. One of the most ominous dangers to the integrity of the American colleges, especially to those of some size and standing, is that they shall become merely a reflection of the national culture, or lack of it; this is true when our society needs and should demand much more of us. There is a strong suspicion in many quarters where thinking about the problem is being done that the colleges of the country are largely populated by the wrong people, and are being warped from their primary intellectual purposes by alien ideals—athletic, social, or financial. For the college should be a model of intellectual communal life, and from that position should show its society a fuller, richer, more gracious way of life.

Upon the surface, the state of our national condition is incredibly propitious and reassuring. Our prosperity since the War has produced a society of huge proportions that in the main is well-fed, well-clothed, well-housed, well-mannered, good-natured —secure for the most part from want and tyranny, with more leisure than ever before in the history of man. Moreover, our society has undertaken to educate all of its young people as far as they can and will go, and there are signs that the society is beginning to recognize its financial responsibilities to education, even at the college and university level. But financial help, however welcome, is not by itself enough. Our ideal of education for all, partially noble in intention and partially merely expedient, has brought many problems in its train. And these problems cry out for a sympathetic understanding. At the present time the quality of our nation's social life seems good. Our national leaders for the most part are men of integrity, idealism, and skill; our literary and artistic people command an international respect such as they never had before; our scientists and engineers, especially the latter, are the wonder and the envy of other nations; our teachers in our colleges and universities are learned and devoted. These groups make up that "dynamic minority" by whose vigor and quality, according to Toynbee, the health of a society is to be judged. But this "dynamic minority" for the most part is the product of our educational system of thirty to forty years ago. Can we look forward to such a happy condition in the future? Our high schools have already been flooded by incompetent pupils, taught by relatively fewer and less competent teachers than formerly. And this is a fate that is looming over our colleges at the present time.

The above rosy view of our culture at present is all too superficial and all too flattering to the actualities of our condition. Far too much, our colleges are mere reflections of our society, microcosms of the great world which supports them; and I think it may be profitable for us to look intently at the college in that light for a few moments.

As we look at our students upon their entrance to college we continue for a moment to live in the rosy glow of optimism. It is probably the experience of all of us that our students come to us with ever increasing intelligence quotients. Why is this? It is hard to believe that our national intelligence is rising so spectacularly. Perhaps we are selecting our students better, with more adequate means of measurement. Or perhaps, as the skeptic might suggest, the clever student has learned to pass our "objective" examinations without the effort of learning anything. But it is soon apparent that in their elementary and high school experience our students have not mastered the basic intellectual tools and skills—they have not learned to think with any accuracy, to read with any comprehension, to write with any precision, or to speak well. Nor have they to any appreciable extent acquired the basic moral and civic virtues, for all their courses in citizenship, so necessary to a society that aims to be democratic and free. They show little respect for law and order, and less concern for their fellow men. They exhibit what has been called a "devastating egalitarianism," and their chief desire seems to be to conform to a low level of mediocrity.

The causes of these conditions seem to be deep-rooted in our society. It is not merely that our schools are flooded by numbers, or that the teachers in the schools are inadequate. These things are so, but the reasons are further to seek. According to Erich Fromm, one of the most profound and excoriating of the critics of our society, the fundamental causes are the industrialization and the urbanization of our lives in our time. From these causes come the alienation of the individual from reality—the distance from actuality of most of our work and life, the quality of abstraction from nature; the specialization of our tasks; and the consequent specialized, divided, and narrow intelligence of our people. He sees in our society a distinct increase since the nineteenth century in stupidity. "Indeed," he says, "we have the know-how, but we do not have the know-why, nor the know-what-for. We have many persons with good and high intelligence quotients, but our intelligence tests measure the ability to memorize, to manipulate thoughts quickly—but not to reason." As a prime example, he cites the new gigantic calculating machines:

> The new automatic brains are indeed a good illustration of what is meant here by intelligence. They manipulate data which are fed into them; they compare, select, and eventually come out with results more quickly or more error-proof than human intelligence could. However, the condition of all this is that the basic data are fed to them beforehand. What the electric brain cannot do is think creatively, to arrive at an insight into the essence of the observed facts, to go beyond the data with which it has been fed. The machine can duplicate or even improve on intelligence, but it cannot simulate reason.

This is to say that our industrialized society is so intent upon production of anything at any cost that it forgets that the important thing is man, the self, the individual, and we are in danger of creating a society of skillful robots. This tendency, so deep in our society and so prevalent in our advertising and propaganda, has profoundly affected our educational system and distorted all of its traditional values. Unfortunately, we have produced no tests or electric brains that will measure reason, ethics, imagination, and compassion in the students that we admit to our colleges. If this criticism is valid, as I believe it to be, our better colleges have the responsibility of making every effort to correct the mass tendency and to make our graduates real three-dimensional persons of wisdom, individuality, and conscience. The world is too much with them, and with us.

No one who has watched the college scene for a number of years can be less than amazed at the energy of the young. Indeed, one is reminded of nothing so much as that fierce activity among Milton's lesser devils in Hell when the grand council has broken up. It is like the students at the end of a dull lecture:

> . . . the rangèd Powers
> Disband; and, wandering, each his several way
> Pursues, as inclination or sad choice
> Leads him perplexed, where he may likeliest find
> Truce to his restless thoughts, and entertain
> The irksome hours . . . .
> Part on the plain, or in the air sublime,
> Upon the wing or in swift race contend. . .
> Part curb their fiery steeds, or shun the goal
> With rapid wheels, or fronted brigads form . . . .
> Others with vast Typhoean rage, more fell,
> Rend up both rocks and hills, and ride the air
> In whirlwind; Hell scarce holds the wild uproar. . . .

Others, more mild,
Retreated in a silent valley, sing
With notes angelical to many a harp
Their own heroic deeds, and hapless fall
By doom of battle, and complain that Fate
Free virtue should enthrall to Force or Chance.
Their song was partial; but the harmony
(What could it less when Spirits immortal sing?)
Suspended Hell, and took with ravishment
The thronging audience. . . .
Others apart sat on a hill retired [These are few]
In thoughts more elevate, and reasoned high
Of Providence, Foreknowledge, Will, and Fate—
Fixed fate, free will, foreknowledge absolute—
And found no end, in wandering mazes lost.

Now what is there in our college programs, or
not in our programs, that makes our students antici-
pate the fierce competitive world of patterned activity in which they are to spend most of their lives?
Is it, possibly, that the studies with which we con-
front them are too theoretical, too far from reality
for them? Why do they so frequently abandon the
leisure and privacy which we ought to provide in
our colleges, for such strenuous preliminary activity? Are they too young to comprehend the significance of literature, science, history, and philosophy?
Or are we overwhelmed by the great corrupt world
of vocation that infiltrates our halls? How can we

protect students from such premature conformity?

These are questions of immediate and major concern to our colleges, but I would like to turn now to a different set, a set that also cripples the college somewhat in the performance of its duties. These difficulties have to do, for the most part, with the college in its relationship to the university which harbors it. It is possible for the dean of a college within the university to look occasionally with longing on the college that has no such ties, that is independent and can shape its own course without restrictions. But, on balance, the college within the university is a richer place and provides a richer experience for its students. There can be no doubt, however, that over the years such colleges have been losing control of their own affairs. Their income is usually handsomely milked to support the less productive parts of the university. The failure of secondary schools and the poor preparation of the students compels the college to devote much time to remedial or elementary work. At the other end of the scale, professional and graduate schools, and professional associations, exert vocational pressures upon the college program. Quite as hampering to the freedom of the college is the rigid departmentalization in the structure of most of our universities. So vested and taken for granted are the controls of the departments that it is frequently impossible to experiment, to introduce new interdepartmental programs into the curriculum. Last, but not least, the departments more and more train the young teachers through the doctors' degrees for the purposes of their own departmental aggrandizement—to what is often an arid scholarship—and give little attention to the needs of college teaching.

But something is happening in our best colleges that should be recorded here. In the past, we have seen the old idea of the class—the recitation—still practiced at places like West Point and the Naval Academy, give way to the lecture as the prevailing mode of instruction, a mode that was perhaps even less effective. It was in this phase of college instruction that the classic definition of the professor was born: "A professor is a man who talks in other people's sleep." But that phase of Germanic teaching is now itself partially on the way out. There will always be a need for some lectures. But at the insistence now of our students, and with the eager agreement of our young teachers, we are developing on a large scale the method of round-the-table discussion—the teacher at the head of the table with eight or ten students eagerly participating. The old classroom with its serried ranks of seats is giving way to the newer mode of instruction that puts upon the student a fair share of the responsibility for his education.

For all the pressures upon it—and I have enumerated only a few—and all its problems, I would like to reaffirm my faith in the liberal college set at the base of the university. The small independent college, unassociated with the university, has its distinct values and uses, and is the right place for many students to mature in. But it cannot provide the range and richness, the substantial culture, or the vision of the great world which seems to be necessary to quite a number, or the rare opportunity for the exceptional student to go far in a special field of his interest. In my position at Yale I have seen many applications for transfer by able students of small but excellent colleges who have, or feel they have, exhausted their local scene by the end of their Sophomore year. If they are accepted these students are often among the best products of the college within the university, and are all the better for their differing experiences in two diverse institutions. At the university the atmosphere is denser and the student will meet more frequently the scholar who has been called "a strange amalgam of social failure, intellectual freak, and political hazard," but is nevertheless a most valuable and influential man in our society. For the university is not infrequently the refuge from society of the lonely, creative mind. To him students may repair and in their golden urns draw light.

But to maintain itself at its best the college must have the proper conditions. Ideally, it must control its conditions of entrance, its curriculum, its budget, and its degrees. I should like to say a word about each of these, leaving my fuller comment upon the curriculum for a later occasion. The colleges are already overcrowded, and are ill-prepared to meet the onrush of students which will be upon us in two or three years. We must scrutinize, and I think curb, our greed and ambitions. One may sympathize with the colleges in the state universities in their almost defenseless position. But we in the independent colleges have an equally important task. More than ever we must be the guardians of standards, and not take on more than we can do thoroughly and well. The alternative is to bog down into a devastating mediocrity—a condition that already threatens higher education in America. Therefore, our standards of admission should be clear and rigorous, and must not yield to expediency and pressure.

The curriculum, too, must be clear and strong against the many pressures that threaten its integrity —the desire of the students for the immediately practical, the pressure of the society for the specialist at too early a stage in his career, the encroaching demands of professional schools and associations. Our goal should be to educate our students for the difficult art of humane and gracious, just and compassionate living—in short, to make magnanimous men and women.

To achieve its ends and to be free to experiment in new directions the liberal college should have at least some small portion of the university budget that is completely its own and not subject to raids from the rest of the university. The practice in most of our universities, as we well know, is for the great maw to swallow the income of the college, and to apportion it to the hungry departments and schools. Being a university man, as well as a college dean, I see the necessity of much of this. Without the support of the college, the graduate school will often be a poor desiccated thing and the university will decline. But without some small independent funds of its own the college is tied to departments and their vested interests, and the college is not free to command the necessary faculty for the interesting experiment that may cut across departmental lines, the bold new program which, though small, may revitalize the intellectual life of the whole college and give it a fresh vision of excellence.

What I plead for is that each college should develop for itself its own native character and personality. To do this it must have clear, well-defined aims and the appropriate methods and corporate life for achieving those aims. How do our various colleges, each in its own way, manage to inculcate to some degree those high moral characteristics in our students which our society so badly needs—independence of judgment, a sense of responsibility, imagination, appreciation, compassion, and faith in principle? We do, somehow, by the grace of heaven and the innate decency of youth. But, we don't succeed too well. Instead, we are likely to give our students a particular stamp—a fairly faithful, but often superficial, reflection of the prevailing climate of our separate institutions. It is often not what the administration or the faculty desires. It is more frequently what the students think of themselves. It is our function to keep before them and see that they get what Whitehead calls "a vision of greatness." It is said that a discerning person can tell a Harvard man, a Yale man, a Princeton man, and I have no doubt, a Tulane man or a Vanderbilt man. There is no doubt that we do stamp a kind of character upon them during their four years—the Harvard man is often an intellectual leader and reads more books, the Yale man is frequently a leader for social improvement in his community. And so, each institution does something to its students. It takes a discerning eye to see differences and I sometimes resort to Gulliver's remark to the effect that the king of Lilliput was a fingernail taller than any of his subjects.

And yet, the climate of opinion—what has been called the campus *ethos*—cannot be so lightly regarded, for it is an extremely important thing. We faculty people are likely to think that we make that climate of opinion, that habit of life and custom, but

I think we largely delude ourselves. We can affect it by our attitudes, by our interests, by our earnestness, by our learning and integrity and the breadth or narrowness of our point of view. We can even create a faculty spirit and *ethos* which will be out of line with the prevailing climate of opinion of the place. To some degree the President and the Deans can affect the habit, custom, and tone of a college, and in the long run by their policies and manner and their total lives they can do much. But in the main the *ethos* is set by the undergraduates and is a traditional matter. In some colleges there is a fierce, though unconscious, pressure to conform. In others there is a more liberal, individualistic spirit—occasionally running wild. In some it is a social error to be seen studying or reading—in others there is an eager discussion of ideas. In some there is the premature worship of worldly success, or a too exact and uncritical imitation in little of the world that the students are too soon to enter. In some the prevailing tone is that of the prematurely blasé and indifferent gentleman who is mannered and finished before he has really begun. It would be indiscreet of me to put names to these climates of opinion, but I could do so, as any of us who travel about a good deal think we are able to do in a fairly short time after we have been on a campus.

And yet, in spite of my pessimistic remarks, I must record that every spring a kind of miracle happens. I have come to expect as a matter of course, though I have no right to do so, to see our Seniors rise to their intellectual opportunities and responsibilities, to catch fire as they write their Senior essays and undertake independent work for themselves. They reach a maturity, and even the Juniors feel an anticipatory quiver of excitement. It is an occasion that makes up all arrears, and gives promise for the future.

Now in our Southern youth it seems to me we have a magnificent opportunity. As I see them, they are gay and spirited, highly intelligent, not too easily persuaded, but malleable—polite and considerate, and eager. They are not, on the whole, infected by many of the prepossessions and sophistications which we encounter in so many of our students in the East.

I should like now to conclude with a few observations upon our alumni and alumnae. We must begin, I think, with a profound sense of obligation to them for their loyalty to their college. It is not always as pure as it might be; it is a pride that sometimes slips over into vanity. It has a strong element of self-regard in it. It is frequently chauvinistic. I have heard the alumni of one institution imply that the alumni of a rival institution had only recently escaped by the grace of heaven from jail, and deserved to be put back in it. In their own college they want to interfere, but less often offer constructive criticism. This loyalty is often sophomoric and reaches no further than the football field. Sometimes it strikes me as a pity that alumni have no higher ideals to engage their enthusiasm and loyalty. But this is to see them at their worst and in a phase that is in process of passing. At their best they give their universities not only generous financial support, but something more precious—their deep love, their time, and infinite care. To direct them so that they become friends instead of tyrants is one of the subtlest problems of the university.

Perhaps the worst that can be said of them is really an indictment of the colleges and the society into which they go. The education we have given them is too often superficial—a vaccination that did not take. Ten years out of college and they seem to have become absorbed into the universal conformity of our material American life. They seem to have lost personality, and have forgotten the aspirations and interests of their days in college.

And then a few years later we see coming to the fore in our national life that "dynamic minority"—that handful of magnanimous men who are the leaders in our society and are increasingly the graduates of our colleges—in statesmanship, in business and finance, in law and medicine, in art and music, in the church, in literary, scientific, and intellectual endeavor of all kinds. And there is in the public an increasingly enthusiastic and mature response to this humane and enlightened leadership. Perhaps, viewing the long perspective of history, we may conclude that "nothing is here for tears, Nothing to wail or knock the breast," but much coming from the colleges that is hopeful for the future.

The Liberating Studies

THE MODERN, full-scale university in America is composed of many schools and studies. In its scope and variety it is something new in the world. It is indeed almost a microcosm of the society it serves. The ideal of Ezra Cornell, announced in 1868 at the founding of the great institution which bears his name, to the effect that he wished to establish a university at which any student might study anything has come to pass in many places in our land. The great universities of Europe made no such ambitious attempt, nor such indiscriminate ones. A European visitor to one of our vast, modern American universities may apply the remark of Beatrice Lillie when she was a passenger on the *Queen Mary*. She asked, "When does this place get to New York?" My object here is to look at the effect of this great expansion on the condition of our studies, especially in the colleges, but extending into more adult phases, and to set up if I can a small program of those studies which I think are indispensable to the liberally educated man or woman, and indeed an indispensable ingredient in the educational structure of our country. In my choices of studies I shall be thought by many to be hopelessly old-fashioned and perhaps reactionary. But it is clear that our expansion in our studies has created a dilemma in education, and we have not yet found a satisfactory formula that will bring into harmony an educational experience for our students—that will prepare them adequately for a rich, full life and make them sober, temperate, thoughtful citizens of the present, and yet not limited by its narrow horizons.

We inherited from Europe, of course, a medieval conception of the scope of the university, and its ideal had not drastically changed by the eighteenth century. A university consisted of four major parts: Divinity, Law, Medicine, and the Arts, including the infant sciences under the head of Natural Philosophy. As our earliest colleges grew from the status of mere fragments of colleges in the nineteenth century into potential, though hardly actual, universities, they added departments and schools of law, divinity, and medicine to their general studies. It is at once noticeable, of course, that many of our largest universities, especially our state universities

which are children of the revolutionary political
philosophy that divided church and state so clearly,
have no divinity schools, and indeed in some of them
it is forbidden to teach religion. Even Cornell with
its universal and sweeping ideal does not have a
school of divinity. Most of the older private or independent universities, evolving through the years
from their origins in a branch of the church, still
have a place for what was once the queen of sciences, but in few places is it still the queen. In our
busy, crowded, secular, practical universities, one
wonders what is next to go, and one sees with mis-
giving that the classics have gone in many places,
and other subjects which were once central are in
poor case. It is the law of change and progress that
useless things shall be discarded, but let us be sure
that they are useless and that what we put in their
places shall be as useful in a profound consideration
of the whole nature and aim of education.

I have no inclination at all to deny the admission
of new learning. In the nineteenth century, we
know, the curriculum of our colleges had become
ossified and sterile and its adherents were inclined to
be belligerent toward the new sciences. Therefore
to accommodate the new sciences new institutes
and schools had to be added. In 1844 Yale added
the Sheffield Scientific School to its number, and
soon afterwards Harvard added Lawrence to its
list. Far from being disastrous, these additions re-

invigorated the old colleges, and in time they were incorporated into the older establishments. They made it easier in later years for the social sciences to take their rightful and formal places in the modern curriculum to round it out to a well-proportioned whole. The sciences and the social sciences had to come into a rounded general plan. But though we take what we desire, we must not snatch it eagerly. In order to get the new sciences into the curriculum, Eliot of Harvard introduced the elective system into the college studies; he disrupted the old set program and made every subject the equal in importance of every other. Eliot did not invent Pandora's box, but he made full use of it, and the example of Harvard spread through the colleges of the country, and thence descended disastrously into our high schools. What might have been a gradual broadening of the curriculum became a revolution, and that fact accounts for much of the chaos in education against which we have been struggling for the last seventy-five years. One of our greatest necessities in higher education is to reach a sound and well-reasoned consensus of opinion concerning the appropriate and right studies for the student in college in his freshman and sophomore years—the basis of his future specialization. It is my purpose here to plead for the inclusion of a group of studies in the program which are generally regarded by the student, and I am afraid by our society, as useless.

As I suggested a few minutes ago in another connection, the university in America has, with some exceptions, accepted the assumption that it should be a microcosm of the society in which it exists. And the most salient and obvious fact about our country seems to me to be its determination to be democratic. This fact, operating not only upon the number, nature, and quality of our students but also upon the scope and character of our universities, has created a type of university which is characteristically American, and is something new in our time and in the Western tradition of universities. This strong and egalitarian movement has had the effect of making all studies of equal value in the eyes of the public, and as a result we have seen in the last three-quarters of a century a tremendous proliferation of schools and departments, most of them designed to meet some practical need of the society without much consideration of their appropriateness to an institution of higher learning. I need mention only the most respectable of these schools: agriculture, business, education, journalism, and nursing, and I shall not mention such courses as hotel management or physical education. These schools, as I say, have risen to meet the needs of our ever more complex society; and assuredly, we need men and women well trained in most of these areas. Certainly these areas are important and the university properly concerns itself with them; but vocational training programs are not educational programs and their net effect is to dilute the quality of the university as they strain to make themselves professions similar to those of medicine, law, and divinity. They are intensely practical, and mirror faithfully the countenance of our society. At that level, they need for the most part no defense, and very little aid. But they take room, time, and resources that the university can hardly spare. More important is the imprint upon their students—for their effect upon the student confined to their care is to narrow the mind and spirit to an early practicality and specialization instead of liberating the individual. I need hardly say that a society made up entirely of the graduates of such training schools would be a very dreary one, and the historian, the philosopher, or the poet, seeing such a society in the whole and in perspective, would find it intolerable. Even if there were no philosophers, historians, or poets, such a society would die of apathy and frustration. Seeing the blight of immediacy and practicality upon our complex and specialized society already present a hundred years ago, but not yet developed as it has since that time, Matthew Arnold, the poet and social critic of industrialized England, analyzed the situation in this manner:

For most men in a brazen prison life,
Where, in the sun's hot eye,
With heads bent o'er their toil, they languidly
Their lives to some unmeaning taskwork give,
Dreaming of nought beyond their prison-wall.
And as, year after year,
Fresh products of their barren labour fall
From their tired hands, and rest
Never yet comes more near,
Gloom settles slowly down over their breast;
And while they try to stem
The waves of mournful thought by which they are
   prest,
Death in their prison reaches them,
Unfreed, having seen nothing, still unblest.

A modern American critic of society (Russell Davenport in *The Dignity of Man*) puts the matter in prose and applies it more directly to our problem:

> From infancy we [Americans] are taught to revere the wonderful achievements of Industrial Man. Our realistic toys, the remarks of our parents about the neighbor's new automobile, the urge that animates everyone we know to acquire more and better extensions (the wheels and claws of Industrial Man)—all this profoundly orients us to a definition of

happiness that can *only* be fulfilled in outer terms. Even our educational system places its final accent on the preparation of young men and women to meet the external trials and challenges of American life. . . . Hence, when choosing their college courses, they concentrate on that which will enable them to do this, whether it be "journalism," "home engineering," or "traffic safety." It seems to them no more than a kind of academic luxury to inquire into the inner meaning of Aeschylus— or even to know who he was.

It is clear that in our colleges we must work out a reconciliation between the multitudinous pressures of our society and the larger and more distant ideals that we, as educators, know will be good for the student and ultimately for the country. It will not be easy; the student will have many reasons why he should not pursue a liberal education. He will not have a long view of his life, and he will point out that such an education comes at a high price in money, time, and freedom, that a so-called liberal education is bookish and theoretical and a denial of all his youthful instincts, that when he graduates with such an education there are no immediate material rewards for him, and no immediate advantages. He cannot employ at once what he has learned, and his training has little transfer value.

The activity of his life has been delayed, rather than hastened. In short, at that stage he will conclude that such an education will have been useless to him. And the mass of men is likely to add to the student's objections to a liberal education that the total concept is a luxury, an aristocratic conception at that, and therefore not consonant with our democratic society.

It is not easy to answer these arguments in terms which youth will understand, but we must try to do so. As elders, we know that nothing is so enormously useful to a full and free life as the liberal studies. Only they satisfy some of the deepest needs of human nature—the need to know which is as old as man himself, the need to experience the great variety of feelings and thoughts in our history and in our present world. They extend our understanding and imagination to the lives of other men and other times, and give us a basis for judgment and choice; they nourish our delight in beauty and noble action. Through the liberal studies we are able to borrow the best standards of other places and other times—the best that has been thought and said. We know that these studies may permeate with their influence all our thought and feeling and action in the days to come.

A philosopher friend of mine is fond of referring to the story that Alcibiades tells in Plato's *Symposium* about a companion of his in a military campaign, a strange, ugly soldier whose immense strength was matched only by the delight he took in thinking—in the play of ideas. " 'One morning,' says Alcibiades, 'he was thinking about something that he could not resolve, and he would not give up, but continued thinking from early dawn until noon —there he stood fixed in thought; and at noon attention was drawn to him, and the rumor ran through the wondering crowd that Socrates had been standing and thinking about something ever since the break of day. At last in the evening after supper, some Ionians out of curiosity . . . brought out their mats and slept in the open air that they might watch him and see whether he would stand all night. There he stood all night as well as the day . . . and with the return of light he offered up a prayer to the sun, and went his way.'" Then, says my friend the philosopher, "The Western world has never been quite the same since this strange figure stood that way in thought. He showed men an ideal city and gave them the key. Even tough campaigners who poked fun at him did so with a puzzled respect, for they knew he had the freedom of that city, and in an instant, from the midst of business or the crowd, could go for refreshment to far places where they could not follow."

The liberal studies are obviously not those to bring immediate monetary success. But they do bring things that money cannot buy. They are the

means to comfort and quiet, and richness of mind—
good in themselves. They mature and free the mind,
and give it understanding and appreciation. They
introduce us to the companionship of the great
masters of the past; they form our taste by the best
standards. They lead us to be self-critical; to find
our place in the world and in history; to think and
speak aright, and to become men and women out
of the ordinary run. As I said a few minutes ago, a
liberal education has been called aristocratic. So it
is, in the realm of taste, and it cannot be otherwise.
New ideas drive out the old ones. In America we
have made a great deal in the last two decades of
the common man. But we learn with consternation
from our psychologists that the average mental age
of our adult population is fourteen years. I think
our democracy can use quite a number of uncommon men and women—indeed, we cannot survive
without them—and I am not afraid of creating an
intellectual elite. Such an elite would be one of
brains and talent, open to all who will and in no
sense an aristocracy of blood or social position, or
wealth. In any case, I would point out that it has
not been the traditional aristocracy that has notably
written our literature or furthered our science and
philosophy. They have not often been the orna-
ments of our culture, and it is not from such aristo-
crats that our ideas have come. The common man
rules in our politics; to let him rule our taste is to

submit to mass suffocation. To allow him to rule in the high offices of our country is to invite disaster; to let him dictate our thoughts is to induce a mediocrity which may be slower in its effects, but in the long run just as disastrous. The liberating studies which are the care and the making of such an elite and which at first glance appear useless, are at last the most useful studies of all.

You have probably been asking yourselves when I would become specific and actually name a few subjects or fields that I regard as liberating to the mind and the spirit—those that in my opinion are essential to a liberally educated person.

As we look at our educational system in America as a whole, I think we must conclude that our high schools are our weakest link. Possibly they have the hardest job to do, since they serve such a vast population of such diverse abilities and interests, and are subject to such colossal pressures from all sides. But when all this is taken into consideration, it still must be said that they are doing an inadequate job in the common fundamentals of sound education. They are not providing the students with the necessary *skills*—the elementary three R's—the linguistic skill involved in reading and writing, not only in the ancient and modern foreign languages (they have long disappeared in many high schools), but in English. The mathematical skill is in even worse condition in our schools. In the circumstances, it is too much to expect at this stage any of the higher skills, such as the power to discriminate between fact and error, to weigh evidence, to estimate values, and to make syntheses. We shall be lucky if we can achieve those skills in college.

If we could rely upon the high schools to do the job that we think is theirs, it would be easy to set a kind of standard curriculum in the college. Briefly, it would be something like this. In the Freshman and Sophomore years in college there would be six prescribed courses, unless the student by excellent work in school has anticipated the main content and substance of some of them. Two of these courses should be in the sciences, neglecting neither the physical nor the biological side, and putting to use the mathematical attainments of the student. Here the student should see the immense importance of the empirical method. Two courses should fall into the social sciences, making the student familiar with the great social institutions of our modern world, and the behavior of men in dealing with them. And two courses should be devoted to the arts and letters, for aspiration, example, and value.

From this base a major field of interest may be selected for the last two years of college, consisting of six or seven courses in a subject or related subjects, capped by a senior essay and by a comprehensive examination, both oral and written. Here the student gains a kind of junior mastery and learns to walk upon his own feet, and has to use what powers of synthesis he has.

This will leave the student room for some six or seven year courses in his college program in which he may repair his deficiencies or, more excitingly, pursue the special things that he has long been curious about, or take a course with that particular professor whom to miss has been to miss one of the great and invaluable experiences of his college days.

Well, this is standard and adequate. But there are other dimensions to a genuinely satisfactory education, to a liberating experience, that I should like to speak of—dimensions both within the subject matter of the curriculum and beyond it. And this takes me into the methods of teaching in the different areas.

I shall speak of dimensions rather than subjects, as you will see, but first I should like to clear the ground by mentioning some studies that are not in their deepest nature or in their characteristic presentation as liberating as others. They are unquestionably excellent for their purpose, but their effect is often to narrow the view and limit the perspective of the person studying them. Professional and pre-professional studies usually suffer from this restricting pressure. If we had world enough and time there is no doubt that such a study as engineering could be made a liberal one. But it would take an extensive and penetrating exploration of the

CHRISTIAN ... LIBRARY
COLUMBIA, MISSOURI

history of the field to make it so. The same may be said of medicine and law, for these studies are not commonly taught in their historical dimension. They look too insistently to the present and the practical. A similar charge may often be made against the practice of some of the sciences, but the more valid charge is against the teaching. The teachers of chemistry and biology, for example, would probably deny the indictment, but men in these fields are often so intent upon current research that they forget the exciting history and the broader philosophical and social significance of their fields. They regard the past in their areas with shame as a maze of errors through which investigators have groped to the present almost perfect state of knowledge. And yet, the march of science, properly seen, from the seventeenth century to the present is one of the noblest accomplishments of the human mind.

The social sciences, too, suffer from a somewhat similar self-limitation; with the notable exception of anthropology they do not usually send the mind ranging over time. Their interest for the most part is on the here and now—the local scene and the present time. In their effort to be as objective as the sciences they mainly describe empirical data, and recoil with horror from all judgments and values. As useful as they are to our society at the moment they suffer somewhat from evanescence, so that their analyses of society and their generalizations, if they are bold enough to make them, may be out of date in a few years.

Now, both the sciences and the social sciences are necessary ingredients to a liberal education in the modern world. For the sciences provide the facts which are the bases of contemporary life and thought, and their methods permeate our lives, and shape the modern mind. Moreover, not to know the main lines of the social sciences is to be blind in the world we live in. In this sense, both have been great liberating forces, freeing us from superstition, ignorance, and parochialism, and bringing our lives out into the daylight. But these are the great modern studies and are in no great danger of being neglected. The studies that I would plead for now are in danger of neglect in many of our schools and colleges, and at first glance offer little of practical value, though their value in liberating the mind and spirit from the present and the local are ultimately of immense use.

You have probably noted my earlier observation that such and such a field had little history, or cared little for its own history. It is my belief that the addition of the historical dimension can go a long way towards making any study a liberating one. This is because through the history of a study we see the human mind and spirit in all its struggles and errors, and in all of its triumphs too. It is the dimension of history rather than the subject itself that is the desirable end, and this dimension may be won in the historical aspect of geology, or in economic history broadly conceived, as well as in the subject of history itself. Or in archaeology and anthropology, as they trace the long slow development of man to his present state; or in biology, properly taught, showing the evolution of life through the ages. These studies, as well as history itself, lend perspective to our lives and soberness to our aspirations. They free us from the insistent present.

A second dimension, crossing the vertical line of history horizontally, is the philosophical one. This is the dimension of breadth, of relationships, of speculation, and also of analysis and value. It is the area of comparison and judgment, of choice and principle, of weighing and pondering, and finally of synthesis, fitting the parts in their proper proportions and order into a satisfying whole. As in the case of the historical dimension, this dimension may be gained in other areas than the subject itself, and may be a synthesis of many subjects. But the student should not miss some experience in grappling with the solutions of the great philosophers and the great religious thinkers themselves as they have faced the problems of our being.

A third dimension in education that may not be neglected without the gravest of losses is the imaginative one. Here literature, art, and music are the necessary studies, and especially literature as most available to all, for they above other studies extend the spirit, enlarge the sympathies, and refresh the mind. Literature, especially poetry by its compact and allusive nature, is often the entering gate that lets the growing spirit into a fuller life than the commonplace world allows, and leads on to wisdom in human relationships, to knowledge of oneself, and to delight. The study of literature must be begun early and continued late. The study of music and art will do something of the same kind, but to my partial mind not so broadly or so permanently, nor by themselves so healthily, or generally.

Now, of course, these are not the whole of a liberal education, and other studies are liberating in their degree; for example, the mastery of a foreign language enlarges our freedom, or some of the social studies make us freer citizens of our own world. We need also the sciences to give us the assurance that we are competent men in our generation, and to provide the necessary underpinning for a modern philosophy of life. But these studies merely bring us up to par; the historical, philosophical, and imaginative dimensions add something beyond, and make us liberated men and women. They add the essential ingredients of the free mind.

For a number of years recently we have seen our better and more alert colleges groping to find the modern equivalent for the old curriculum which was disrupted by the flood of new learning of the nineteenth century and the elective system which was its consequence. General education is an attempt to adjust our procedures to the new forces in the world—democracy, which I name first, vast new areas of knowledge, and new methods of instruction. We have seen in our time Columbia, Chicago, Yale, and Harvard each come up with programs, and each sure for a little while that it had the answer. These places have had their imitators in the country, but after a little time these followers have often reverted to the more practical and immediate programs which provide the student with information and training which he can use on the job as soon as he takes his degree.

But the problem remains with us, and so does the ideal that would discipline the mind and personality of the student for a longer and richer conception of living. The program of studies should be more, much more, than adequate for the humdrum business of getting a living. We must train some of our young people to a magnanimous view of life—of its possibilities and responsibilities, what *might be* without losing the sense of *what is.* For our democracy needs leaders of a highly knowledgeable, imaginative, and judicious kind; and where will they come from if not from our colleges? And we must remember, as John Stuart Mill reminds us, that "Men are men before they are lawyers, or physicians, or merchants, or manufacturers; and if you make them capable and sensible men, they will make themselves capable and sensible lawyers or physicians." We need "philosophic lawyers—who demand and are capable of apprehending principles, instead of merely cramming their memory with details."

The prosperity of the country since the close of the Second World War and the prospects of the future give the independent colleges today a magnificent opportunity to make a long stride forward. We have the possibility now of making our terms of admission stiff and discriminating; from our long lists of applicants we can select the students who are well qualified by ability and desire to pursue a humane education as their first aim in being at the university; we can if we choose educate an elite of talent without offense to the principles of democracy. We need not fear that we are creating an aristocracy or a group in any way dangerous to the country. The student today is less conscious of his superiority to his fellow man, and is more conscious of the variety of his associates and his responsibility to the commonwealth. Our American students seem to me to be profoundly committed to the democratic principle. What we need to emphasize with them now is that they can afford the time and energy to make themselves large-minded men and women, magnanimously educated for service to their country in whatever capacity they find themselves.

The University and the
National Culture

IN THIS concluding lecture I wish to speak about
the relation of the university to the national culture in our country and in our time. It will be my
thesis, to state it baldly, that with the coming of the
age of science in its full development to the Western world and the accompanying rise of intense nationalism in our own time, the rise of the United
States to pre-eminence among the nations, and the
universal desire for higher education, especially in
America, the universities of the country have become the preservers of our culture, the advancers
of our learning, to some extent the moulders of the
ideas and standards we live by, the imperfect arbi-
ters of taste, and the pride of the nation. This is a
large assertion and needs defense and explanation.

If my contention is valid, as I believe it is, the
universities have assumed a very grave responsi-

bility. I need only refer to the decisive part played by men from the universities in World War II, not only in developing the weapons of war, but in the conduct of the country in that dangerous time in other respects. The universities, their professors and graduates, have become the brains of the country, and in some respects its conscience. This is true in other countries as well as in America, for out of the English universities came radar and penicillin— a diverse pair—and out of the German universities there would have come weapons more terrible than those we had ready at the time if Hitler had not destroyed, driven out, or crippled the talent originally available to him. As it has developed in the nineteenth and twentieth centuries, in Europe and America, the university has been closely associated with the government, and must serve the purposes of the state. To some extent it must formulate and express the mind and spirit of the nation. It must, beyond its ancient function of perpetuating our inherited store of knowledge—its teaching function—increase knowledge of all kinds as a principal task of its existence. It has become the major institution in society in caring for, criticizing, and advancing our total culture.

I may remind you that the universities were by no means always so central to the national life, nor were they always the almost exclusive headquarters of learning. In the seventeenth and eighteenth centuries many of the greatest minds in the history of Western thought had little or no association with universities. I need mention only a few—Bacon, Spinoza, Descartes, Leibniz, Hobbes, Newton, Boyle, Locke, and Lavoisier. Indeed, during the Age of Enlightenment the world of science, literature, and the arts flourished beyond the walls of the universities. One need only look at the universities of England in the eighteenth century to see how low was the estate of learning in them. The training for the Church, Law, and Medicine had become a farce. As late as 1831 Sir William Hamilton could write these words: "England is the only Christian country, where the Parson, if he reach the University at all, receives the same minimum of Theological tuition as the Squire;—the only civilized country where the degree, which confers on the jurist a strict monopoly of practise, is conferred without either instruction or examination; the only country in the world, where the Physician is turned loose upon society, with extraordinary and odious privileges, but without professional education, or even the slightest guarantee for his skill."

Of course, there were always a few devoted scholars at Oxford and Cambridge, but the idea that the university is peculiarly the center of research and postgraduate training had hardly dawned in England or America before the third quarter of the nineteenth century. Perhaps the best that can be said for the English universities in the eighteenth century, and for their children—the colleges in America—is that there were often in attendance young men of very considerable general ability and moral earnestness. They had to acquire their special competences elsewhere, usually in experience itself.

It was in the nineteenth century that the universities regained the high rank they had held in the Middle Ages. It was in this century that they came to be regarded as the prime repositories of human knowledge, and with the rise of nationalism they took on the new role of being the embodiment of the national mind. Late in the century, and continuing with redoubled strength into the twentieth century, the university, often under the dominance of the state, assumed the further role of being an institution dedicated to the cause of extending the bounds of knowledge. As we shall see, this was especially true in Germany. It was not enough under the new political, economic, and cultural complexities of modern civilization for them to be merely repositories and perpetuators of knowledge. They became the great research centers of the nation, creatures of the state to help invent its weapons, advise its economy, shape its philosophy and its attitude and significance in the world. As such, they are powerful instruments for good or evil in the hands of those who control them.

It was as the expression of the national mind, the

perpetuators of knowledge, and the transmitters of it, but above all as the advancers of knowledge that the German universities won their undisputed pre-eminence in the nineteenth century. It is surprising to see how late many of the great and influential German universities were founded. The University of Berlin, which was perhaps the greatest force in the new conception, was founded in 1810, and Breslau and Bonn about the same time, and one by one the older universities of the country adopted the new conception. They grew with the new German state after the Napoleonic wars, and affected the temper of the new nation. It was the notion of the university as the discoverer and generator of new knowledge that fostered the new philosophers and scholars, such as Kant, Wolff, Fichte, Schelling, Schleiermacher, and Hegel, at first specializing in the humanities as these names indicate, but later in the century moving on to an equal or even greater eminence in the sciences. It was after the example and under the impetus of the German universities that the English established the University of London in 1828, and about the same time the ancient University of Paris was revivified. And ultimately even Oxford and Cambridge and the older universities (so called) of America felt the profound effect of the German example. But more of that later.

The new idea of the university which brought such grandeur to the German universities had in it a number of difficulties which have been disclosed only in our own time. A few of these need comment. By becoming instruments of the state—a strong national state—the universities in the course of time gave up the principle of the universal conception of learning and knowledge and, indeed, surrendered their freedom to pursue knowledge freely and to teach as freely. If this seems too strong a statement, I ask you to look at the result in Russia in its full and logical development where we have Soviet science, Soviet philosophy and Soviet history. Signs of this tendency were apparent in German scholarship late in the nineteenth century, and led German scholars into a chauvinistic and dangerous interpretation of anthropology and history, moving through the Superman to the Nordic. Even in such an innocent area as literature many Germans became convinced that the German translation of Shakespeare was superior to the original, or perhaps that the bard was himself a German. But we may lay no flattering unction to ourselves. We have seen in our time and country how an ardent and parochial nationalism has absorbed much of our research energy, and has openly attacked the freedom of inquiry and teaching in our universities and colleges.

There are other dubious consequences in the modern conception of the university. I am thinking especially of strong and continuing trends towards specialization. This trend is a consequence of many pressures—chiefly the immense increase in our supply of data, which itself rises from the unremitting search for new knowledge. In accepting the idea that its chief task was the advancement of knowledge, the university identified itself with learning, and after that the departmentalization of knowledge was inevitable. Gone were the days when Francis Bacon could take all knowledge for his province. Learning, by the late nineteenth century, had become a specialized vocation of the university scholar and scientist, and the learned man had become the equivalent of the research scholar. Furthermore, specialization played into the hands of nationalism, and knowledge has become more and more a possession of a nation. It is an act of treason when a scholar of one country discloses his secret and individual knowledge to a scholar of another country. In our dangerous world this is a matter of self-preservation. But it was not always so in happier and more innocent times. This is true now of more things than atomic secrets. The consequence is that the university has become the servant of the state, and learning has ceased to be a common human possession. I need hardly remind you that as a consequence of excessive specialization our teaching has been stultified in almost every area of learning. We are thus in danger of perpetuating our troubles and preparing for a fierce and sterile future.

As a result of two great wars and the tides of modern history the American university has now taken, and will take more in the future, the place of intellectual primacy in the world. The universities in Germany are in a desperately weakened condition, and they are hardly stronger in France and Italy and Spain. There is the continuing strong thirst for knowledge in Germany, but many of the professors were exiled in Hitler's time, the students are decidedly less well prepared for their tasks, and there are large areas of ignorance because of inadequate libraries and poverty. So exiled professors report. It is true that there is still considerable vigor in the English universities, but the burden upon the society is possibly too great to be carried for long. Whether we like it or not; whether we are ready or not, now and even more in the future the free world will look to us for leadership in learning and culture. What we do and will do is of immense importance. But since we are the inheritors of the burden of modern learning in the main, it behooves us to look at our American universities in their growth and in their present state—their growth, because only by looking at the history of higher education in America may we understand the diversity of structure and function in our many institutions.

Our heritage from England in the beginning was not the university, nor the university idea. Indeed, it was not even a full college, but rather a fragment

CHRISTIAN COLLEGE LIBRARY
COLUMBIA, MISSOURI

of a collegiate institution. This was the nature of Harvard, Yale, and William and Mary in the colonial days. We have to remind ourselves that it was almost 250 years after the founding of Harvard, and 150 years after the founding of Yale, before those institutions began to take the shape of the modern American university. And the question has been asked a number of times, Why were we so slow in the process? The reasons, I think, are numerous and varied. In the first place, our rather simple agrarian society in the colonies in the early eighteenth century did not demand the specialists who are so essential to a complex industrial society. Furthermore, there was severe competition, and a scattering of our resources; the distances in our country encouraged the rise of small local institutions to serve the widely separated communities. Again, the religious differences in our population made for the establishment of small denominational colleges. Yale is proud of a title which it has awarded itself—The Mother of Colleges—and indeed when we celebrated our 250th anniversary in 1951, there were 41 colleges and universities present as our children. A great many of these, indeed, if not most of them, were founded before Yale became a university itself. A good many of them were founded—and this is a curious fact about higher education in America—before there was a reasonable system of elementary and secondary education in their communities. Finally, in the state of education in England and on the Continent in the eighteenth century there were no university models within the range of vision of the people of the early years of the Republic. The great day of the university in America had to wait for a number of events —the rise of nationalism and wealth in the country, the spread of democracy, the effect of the Scientific and Industrial Revolutions, the physical expansion of the population westward, the freedom of the mind of the nation from the bonds of religious authority, and the model of the university from Europe, mainly provided by Germany in the nineteenth century.

By the end of the first quarter of the nineteenth century a number of our Eastern institutions—Harvard, Yale, Columbia, and Pennsylvania—had some of the necessary ingredients of a university, but hardly yet the point of view. They were little clusters of schools and institutes. Indeed, just after the Revolution the University of Pennsylvania and Harvard had assumed the somewhat pretentious title of university, and presently the University of Virginia was founded under the guidance of Thomas Jefferson. In the South, Georgia and presently North Carolina began to rise. The substance in all these was mainly lacking though the title was honored. There were rather feeble law, medical, and divinity schools, somewhat loosely attached to these colleges. It has been commonly recognized, however, that the first decade after the close of the War between the States, that is, from about 1866 to 1876, was the great early flowering of the university idea in America. In this decade a surprising number of extremely able men in higher education began to appear. Eliot was revolutionizing Harvard; from Yale went White to help in the founding of Cornell, and Gilman to establish Johns Hopkins, and Barnard to resuscitate Columbia; the older Angell was busy at Michigan. In 1867 through the Morrill Act the Land Grant colleges rose, and in the decade of 1880 Minnesota and Wisconsin began to develop as universities. In 1890 the University of Chicago was inaugurated by Harper, another refugee from Yale, and in 1891 Stanford started on its career. By this time James Bryce thought he could recognize eight to twelve true universities in the country and from thirty to forty institutions that would qualify as undergraduate colleges, whatever they called themselves. The pattern of the university world of America had taken its present shape by 1900, though it would be a mistake to think of American universities as fully mature at this date.

The Eastern colleges, begun as fragments of Oxford and Cambridge, through the nineteenth century gradually made themselves universities by a process of agglomeration. The newer universities which were founded in the last quarter of the century were almost pure products of the German idea of a university; that is, clusters of professional schools in law, medicine, and the higher arts and sciences, where the student could study what he pleased, and where the professors were free to teach, to lecture, to investigate and publish, and above all to compete with each other in the discovery of new knowledge. In the history of the university in America the German example and influence was the most important element. It is a well-known fact that many of our most distinguished and university-minded professors of that time were trained in Germany. Even the older Eastern universities were profoundly affected by the German ideal, and grafted upon the English model of a residential undergraduate college the higher graduate and professional schools. We were at that time still in a colonial position in higher education in relation to Europe. And the question naturally arises, Where are we now? It is a question I must try to answer.

We found much in the German models that suited the American temperament, notably the immediate and utilitarian impulses of their training for the professions, their practical applications of knowledge to the world of industrial and national strength, and the competitive search for new knowledge. This is not to deny our native powers of invention, or reinvention. Indeed inventiveness may be called our great forte; so far in history we have generally been content to let Europe produce the great seminal ideas, and we have been satisfied if we could adapt their ideas to some practical use. Our civilization and culture are so far more Roman than Greek, strong in the arts of engineering and less adequate in the world of creation. We have emerged from the colonial stage in our culture and learning, but candor compels me to say that we have not yet attained our full independence. We have had in our history a long line of inventors and appliers, but relatively few of the great minds. We have had a few giants among the creators, such as Willard Gibbs in the physical sciences, and James and Dewey in philosophy. In literature, art, and music we have barely come of age. Perhaps in architecture we are further advanced. These things, rather than the "standard of living" in the usual sense of that phrase, measure the quality of a civilization or a culture.

Now when we look at the "Kings of Modern Thought" we find that most of them are still European, the products of European and English universities. In the biological and psychological sciences the great names are Pavlov, Freud, and Jung; in the physical sciences Einstein and Bohr; in economics, J. M. Keynes, an Englishman; in history Spengler and Toynbee; in philosophy Bergson and Whitehead; in religious thought Kierkegaard, Barth, Maritain, and Sartre; in architecture Gropius. Many of

these men are dead, but their influence is still domi-
nant. The remainder are elderly. But they are the
products of European universities and European
culture, and it is the Indian summer of that culture.
We in America have not yet achieved the ultimate
grandeur of the modern university; that is, the production of great germinal minds.

The American scholar and scientist is an admi-
rable man—knowledgeable, conscientious in the
highest degree, usually modest concerning his accomplishments, and altogether a competent man in
his generation and his profession. He is not yet the
great man, and "Great men," as Edmund Burke
tells us, "are the guideposts and landmarks in the
state." He is still a follower, an adapter, rather than
a creator, or a master. The truth is that with some
exceptions he is too often a disciple, still a student
of greater men. I look forward most eagerly to the
time, which I shall hardly live to see, when our country will produce the great scientist, the great archi-
tect, the great philosopher, and this nation will be
recognized as the home of learning in the new age.

This is the task which our universities in America
must aspire to perform: As the chief custodians of
our culture they must themselves have a vision of
greatness; they must "raise the intellectual tone of
society, cultivate the public mind, purify the national taste, supply true principles to popular aims

and fixed aims to popular aspiration, give enlargement and sobriety to the ideas of the age, facilitate the exercise of political power, and refine the intercourse of private life." So we return to Newman's conception. But now we must add the further heavy duty: The university must originate the new ideas by which our society and the world must progress. Given time, I believe we shall be equal to the challenge.

But this will ask for a better society than we have now—such a society as Pericles suggested Athens to be. And we need better arrangements for our potentially great men of learning. We need to free them from part of the heavy burden of instruction of students which we have put upon all our teachers; we need to free our scientists from the burden of contractual research; we need to provide them with leisure and with the means to take their part in the great forward march of mind in our long tradition. Within the context of our democracy we must recognize the place and importance of the uncommon man. Though we should never let the great professor and specialist take the important and dangerous place that he assumed in Nietzsche's Germany, we must nevertheless reconcile democracy to intellectual quality.

Date Due

OCT 2 2 1957		
DEC 1 6 1957		
1 Day RVE ambert		
⑤ PRINTED	IN U. S. A.	